IN MY FATHER'S LAND

RHONDA POWELL

WESTBOW
PRESS®
A DIVISION OF THOMAS NELSON
& ZONDERVAN

Copyright © 2015, 2016 Rhonda Powell.

All rights reserved. No part of this book may be used or reproduced by any means, graphic, electronic, or mechanical, including photocopying, recording, taping or by any information storage retrieval system without the written permission of the author except in the case of brief quotations embodied in critical articles and reviews.

Author photo by J. New Photograph

WestBow Press books may be ordered through booksellers or by contacting:

WestBow Press
A Division of Thomas Nelson & Zondervan
1663 Liberty Drive
Bloomington, IN 47403
www.westbowpress.com
1 (866) 928-1240

Because of the dynamic nature of the Internet, any web addresses or links contained in this book may have changed since publication and may no longer be valid. The views expressed in this work are solely those of the author and do not necessarily reflect the views of the publisher, and the publisher hereby disclaims any responsibility for them.

Any people depicted in stock imagery provided by Thinkstock are models, and such images are being used for illustrative purposes only. Certain stock imagery © Thinkstock.

ISBN: 978-1-5127-4016-5 (sc)

Library of Congress Control Number: 2016906853

Print information available on the last page.

WestBow Press rev. date: 08/30/2016

Chapter 1

You would have thought that after working as a physician's assistant in the medical field, I would have known something was wrong with my body. I thought I had a busted eardrum or maybe some wax buildup in my ear, a cold, or any of a number of short-term hearing problems—anything but what it actually was. I was so worried about making a living for my children and me that it almost cost me my life.

I was working at a restaurant, putting myself thru EMT (emergency medical technician) school when I first noticed that I couldn't hear in my left ear. I wasn't about to tell anyone that I was deaf in one ear; that could ruin my chances of becoming an EMT. As long as I could do what needed to be done safely, I was fine.

At that time in my life, my three children and my job kept me so busy I was always on the go. I didn't have time to worry about some little medical problem like a busted eardrum. Besides, it didn't hurt and I really thought my hearing would come back. Once again I was wrong. It never would.

After finishing school I was licensed as an EMT and went to work for a doctor in a neighboring town. That is where I became a licensed physician's assistant. But I still needed to be certified as a nursing aide. With all the licenses and certifications I had, I was still required to obtain a CNA certificate so I could work in the home health field. Home health had become a growing industry and the money was there to be made. A home health agency would be a really good career move for me. I could triple my income and move out on my own. I wouldn't need my ex-husband's or my mother's help. I would be able to support my children and me. I took the CNA class at the local hospital in my hometown and got my certification. Now that I had all three licenses, I could apply for and get the job that I had worked so hard for.

While I was attending school at the hospital, I met a woman named Ruthie. Her brother planned to open a home health agency in our area, and he needed to hire someone to help run the agency as well as take care of the patients. I really wanted that job. I applied for the position and got it! I finally got the job I had wanted. I had worked hard for all my licensees and certificates, and now I would make some decent money. I was one happy person.

After working for a few weeks to get the agency up and running, we got our first patients. I was so excited. A couple of weeks after that, I had a full day of patients to visit. I loved my job. I finally felt as though I was doing something good with my life.

A year passed and the home health agency was doing great. I was certainly doing well at my job. I had gotten a raise, and I couldn't have asked for better people to work for. My schedule was hectic, but I loved it. And the money I was making wasn't too shabby either. I was caught up on my bills and was buying a small, two-bedroom mobile home for my children and me. We were finally going to be able to move into our own home. Just thinking about the move made me happy.

I started noticing that sometimes I would get light-headed and at least once a week I would have a headache. I thought the headaches were stress related. Lord knows I had plenty in my life to be stressed about—three young and very busy children plus trying to move, not to mention all the bills. My youngest was a baby girl, who had just started private preschool. As most parents will tell you, there is no time to be sick when you have children. It never occurred to me that my problems were because of my left ear, which never bothered me. My right ear seemed to have taken over for my deaf left ear, so I never really noticed a difference. I thought I was in good health other than my allergies, which were controlled with medication.

I ignored the dizziness I was having because it was more like being light-headed. And the light-headedness didn't last very long. It usually passed quickly. I always thought that was due to my allergies, which were horrible. It seemed as though I was allergic to everything.

One day my boss, Freddie, said he would like to offer some of our patients a free hearing test, so he had me ask my patients if they would like to come by the agency for the test. Freddie was always thinking about improving the health and welfare of our clients, and we were always promoting wellness checkups. So it wasn't unusual for him to do something like this for our patients. On the day of the hearing test, I brought Mrs. Dottie into the office. She was such a fun person to be around. She always talked about her younger days and all the fun she'd had as a teen.

Mrs. Dottie was anxious about having her hearing tested. Seeing how nervous she was, I told her I would take the test first, and she could go after me. I had forgotten about my own hearing loss until I placed the earphones onto my head. My concern was to get my patients' hearing checked, and the only way to get her hearing tested was if I went first. Smart, huh?

The gentleman who was performing the hearing test began to explain how the test worked. I was to point to the ear that I heard the sound in. When I was in school, they tested our hearing exactly the same way every year, so I knew how it worked.

I heard every sound with my right ear; however, I didn't hear anything in my left ear. Not one beep. After I finished the test, he looked into my ears and sat back down in his chair.

"When did you notice that you couldn't hear in your left ear?" he asked me.

I answered him with a shrug of my shoulders. I didn't want to answer that question. I thought to myself, *I'm not here for me.*

"The hearing in your right ear is fine, but you're totally deaf in your left ear," he said. "It looks like there is something behind your eardrum." He couldn't tell what it was. "Whatever it is, it's most likely the cause of your hearing loss."

He advised me to see my family physician as soon as I could. My doctor would be able to run a test to tell me exactly what it was.

Since Ruthie was standing there and heard what the examiner told me, she suggested that she could call my doctor and make an appointment. She knew my personal physician very well; our home health agency took care of his homebound patients. And since our office was just a couple of doors down from his, we had gotten to know the doctor and his nurses quite well.

"Ruthie, that would be great," I said as I left.

I needed to take Mrs. Dottie back home. I thanked Ruthie once again and told her I would call her as soon as I dropped off Mrs. Dottie. However, before I got into Mrs. Dottie's driveway, my pager started beeping. It was the office, so I called Ruthie as soon as I got into Mrs. Dottie's house. Ruthie had already called the doctor's office and made an appointment for me. I didn't know what she said to the girls in the doctor's office, but they made my appointment for that afternoon. I couldn't believe Ruthie had gotten me in that quickly.

"Ruthie, I said I still have a couple of patients left to visit. Would it be okay if I went to see them in the morning?"

"No!" Ruthie said. "You need to go now."

She insisted that she would find someone to take care of my patients so I could go that afternoon.

"No excuses," she said. "Go now!"

Ruthie knew I was nervous so before she hung up the phone, she said, "It's going to be okay, Casey. I'm praying for you."

I left Mrs. Dottie's house and went straight to my doctor's office. I hated going to the doctor. I was the one who was always telling everyone, "You need to go see the doctor," but I never took my own advice.

Chapter 2

When I walked into Dr. Mills's office, his receptionist, Sadie, told me the doctor knew that I was coming to see him and he was expecting me. "Follow me into the back, Casey," she said, leading me down a short hallway.

I followed her into one of the examining rooms in the back of the office. The exam room reminded me why I always hated to see the doctor. The starch-white walls; the examination table against the far wall, draped in its paper sheet; and the large, round clock on the wall ticking away the time made me want to run!

"Sit in here," Sadie said, smiling at me. "The doc will be in to see you in just a few minutes." She waited a moment, observing me, and then said, "Try to relax, Casey. We are going to take good care of you."

"Thank you, Sadie," I said.

But there was no way I could relax, not until this was over with. I had been ignoring this for a while. Now that it was all coming to a head, I had to deal with it. I was scared. What if there was something wrong, something that a shot of antibiotics couldn't fix? I was so nervous that when I looked down, I saw my foot shaking uncontrollably. I pressed it down hard on the floor so it would stop. I kept telling myself, *Everything is going to be okay. Calm down. You're making too much out of this.*

A young girl I'd never met before came into the room. She took my vital signs and asked me why I had come to see the doctor. I told her about my hearing test and that it was most likely just some wax buildup. But as I explained to her what was happening, it hit me that something was actually wrong with me. I never wanted to admit that I had a problem. She wrote what I said onto my chart along with my vital signs, and then she turned to me with a smile and said softly, "Dr. Mills will be in to see you shortly." Then out the door she went. Sadie had trained her quite well.

It wasn't long before the doctor came into the room. He was always smiling and teasing me about bringing him a key-lime pie, his favorite. He reminded me of Santa Claus, always rosy cheeked with his glasses sitting below the bridge of his nose.

"So what's going on, kid?" he asked.

"Well, Doctor, I took a hearing test earlier today at work and I failed it. I didn't hear anything in my left ear. However, I heard fine in my right ear. Doc, I haven't been able to hear in my left ear for a long time. At least for the past two years."

When I told him how long it had actually been since I had lost my hearing, he got upset. "You really have to take better care of yourself," Dr. Mills said. "How are you going to take care of others if you don't take care of yourself?"

He began to look into my ear and then said, "I'm going to take X-rays of that ear, Okay?"

"Sure," I said, "if that is what you need to do. I'm sure it's nothing, Dr. Mills. That's why I never said anything about it before. Besides, my ear doesn't hurt! Wouldn't it hurt if there was something wrong with it?"

"I don't know what it is, Casey, but I'm going to find out," he replied.

Then he sent me across the hall to get the X-ray's.

After taking the X-rays, the technician told me, "Dr. Mills will have the X-rays in just a little while. Then he can read them and give you the results."

"Thank you," I said.

Then the technician sent me back across the hall to the doctor's office.

When I walked back into the waiting area, Sadie waved at me to follow her to the back. She brought me straight into Dr. Mills's office instead of an examination room.

"As soon as we get the results back, he will be in to go over them with you. Just sit tight," Sadie said. "It shouldn't take much longer."

It couldn't have been there more than fifteen minutes when Dr. Mills came into the room. This time he wasn't smiling. He sat in his chair. He never looked up at me until he wheeled directly in front of me.

"Casey, I think we found the problem," he said.

Without hesitating, he began to tell me what he had found.

"It's a mass behind your eardrum; it's located in your left ear canal. I'm going to send you to an ENT—an ear, nose, and throat specialist—immediately. The doctor is here in town. He is a good doctor, and I trust his opinion. I would like him to take a look at you. I can have Sadie make the appointment for you if you'd like. I want him to see you as soon as he can. The sooner the better! As soon as we get this appointment made with him, I want you to go see him. Don't put this off, Casey. Okay?"

"Okay, Doc." That was all I could manage to say.

"Casey, I'm sorry," he said.

I was in total shock. My mind was still stuck on the word *mass*. Dr. Mills had to repeat everything he said to me. After he repeated everything to me for the second time, I shook my head in agreement.

"I promise, Dr. Mills, I will go see the ear, nose, and throat doctor."

As I was leaving the examining room, Sadie met me in the hallway. "Casey, I called the ear, nose, and throat doctor. He said for you to come in this afternoon," Sadie said. "Please let us know what the doctor has to say."

"I will, Sadie, I will!"

I remember thinking, *He wants to see me right now? Why? I don't feel sick. I just can't hear in one ear.*

Chapter 3

I don't remember the drive to the ENT's office, but I do remember there was a ton of paperwork to fill out. And the nurse asked me a lot of questions. All I wanted was to get this over with. There was no way this could be happening to me. *I'm not sick; I don't feel sick.*

I remember the first time I saw Dr. Kim. He came in smiling with his hand held out to shake mine. That put me at ease for a few minutes. He was a small Oriental man with a soft voice. He told me that he had spoken to Dr. Mills about my hearing loss, and Dr. Mills had told him about finding a mass in my left ear. He wanted to know if I would agree to a few other tests.

"I would like to have an MRI, a CAT scan of your brain, and also a blood test. Can you do them first thing in the morning?" Dr. Kim asked. "It's important to get these tests done as soon as possible. If this is a mass, we need to take action immediately."

"Yes," I said, "I can have the test done first thing in the morning. That will be fine, Dr. Kim."

Leaving the doctor's office, I was in a daze. When I managed to get into my car, I froze. I sat inside of my car and cried. I don't know how long I sat there. I was in shock! I was shaking and sick to my stomach. I couldn't believe this was happening to me. I remember asking God, "Why?" I screamed out loud, "Why is this happening to me, Lord?" Then immediately afterward, I felt guilty for asking him why. All my life I had been told that you should never question God, that he has a reason for everything, and it's not your place to question him.

I went straight home and cried for the rest of the day. I wanted so badly to tell someone what was happening to me. But who? And besides, I didn't know for certain if I had a tumor in my brain. *I will just wait till I know for sure*, I thought.

That night I didn't say anything to anyone, not even to my best friend, about what my doctor had found on the X-ray's. I kept it to myself. My ex-husband, D. B., whom I still lived with (until I could afford to get a place of my own), had gotten a job and worked nights. At least he wouldn't be home to argue with, and I didn't think he would believe me anyway. He never believed anything I told him. Maybe I would have some peace and quiet, and maybe I could get some sleep. That would be a blessing.

I didn't fall asleep that night until the wee hours of the morning. I kept thinking about what the doctors had told me. And when I closed my eyes to fall asleep, I could see and hear Dr. Mills as he told me there was a mass in my brain. I kept telling myself, *You're not sick; you're not going to die. It's all been a mistake.* After tossing and turning in bed half the night, I finally fell asleep.

Chapter 4

I woke up the next morning to the alarm clock going off at five o'clock. I didn't want to get up because I felt so depressed. I just wanted to stay in bed all day. I forced myself out of bed and into the shower. I threw my hair into a ponytail. I didn't bother putting on my makeup. I didn't feel like doing anything but crying. I got the kids up, made them breakfast, and got them ready for school. I dropped my daughter off at day care around six thirty and headed for my first patient's house, forgetting that I had to go to the hospital for testing. Well, actually I didn't forgot at all; I was trying to forget! I didn't want to know the truth. If I said I forgot about the testing, maybe I could at least put it off for a few more days.

When I arrived at my patient's home, I came back to reality. I had to go to the hospital for testing; I needed to know the truth and deal with it. *I have a mass in my head? I'm going to die!* They never said I was going to die, but deep down inside I felt it.

I took care of my patient as if nothing was wrong with me. We talked and laughed the whole time I was there. I guess that's just what a caregiver does. We hide our own hurts so we can take care of everybody else. By ignoring our own pain, we think it will go away. I had always heard that doctors and nurses make the worst patients. I guess it's true because only after I had finished with my patient's care did I go to the hospital. I was running late for the test, but that would have to be okay. Maybe they would have to put the testing off for another day or two, or maybe they wouldn't need to run any tests. When I got there, they might tell me it was all a big mistake. I felt so alone. I noticed as I got closer to the radiology department, I began to tremble again and that made me mad at myself. I had been told most of my life that I always made something out of nothing, and this was probably one of those times. My mother always told me to suck it up. That's why I hadn't told anyone what was going on with me. I didn't want to hear their condescending tones. Not my mom and certainly not my ex-husband. I hadn't even told my friend. I would wait to tell them after I heard what the doctor told me. I wanted to know exactly what it was before I said anything to my family. Actually I didn't know what I was going to tell them, or if I would tell them.

I remember the first time I had an MRI (magnetic resonance imaging). I was scared to death. The machine was so big and loud. It was so loud they gave me earplugs. They strapped my head down to the table so it wouldn't move during the testing. I felt as if I was going to suffocate. The machine was open on one end and closed on the other. It didn't matter because I couldn't see out anyway. So remember, if you're claustrophobic you need to let your doctor know. Now they have what is called an open-air MRI. It's so much easier. It's still noisy but not too bad. And some places even have music you can listen to during the testing

Next was the blood test. I had given blood before so I knew what to expect. No big deal. However, I don't like needles; they make my stomach feel queasy. So I just look the other way when they start taking my blood. It didn't hurt; I just didn't like it, but I got through it. They took several vials of blood.

Then the nurse sent me back down the hall for a CT scan. The CT scan was more like an X-ray and didn't take long. It was painless and not scary at all.

When I was finished with all the testing, I was told that Dr. Kim would call me as soon as he got the results. He had ordered the tests to be done STAT, so he would have the results of the MRI and CT scan sometime that afternoon. The blood test would take up to seventy-two hours. I left the hospital and went back to work.

I still was not telling anyone what I was going through, but I was crying between patients. The only one who knew anything about what was happening to me was Ruthie, our office manager at the home health agency. She had been there when I took the hearing test, and it was her job to make sure that someone was going to cover my patients at work for me. Soon I'd know the truth.

Chapter 5

That afternoon my pager started to buzz. Someone was paging me from a phone number I didn't recognize. Since I didn't recognize the number, I thought it was most likely Dr. Kim's office calling me to tell me they had gotten the results back from the testing. I didn't return the call right away. Instead I put the pager back into my pocket. To tell you the truth, I was scared. I didn't want to know what they found. However, within a few minutes, Ruthie began to page me. I saw it was Ruthie and put the pager down into the console of my car. I didn't want to hear it. Then Ruthie started paging me with a 911 message. Anytime she paged with a 911, everyone who worked at the agency knew to call the office immediately, that there was an emergency. But I knew why she was paging me.

When I arrived at my next patient's home, it had been a half an hour since Ruthie had paged me. My patient told me that Ruthie had tried to call me and she wanted me to call her at the office as soon as possible. When Ruthie answered the phone, I could tell immediately that she was upset with me. Ruthie was like everyone's mother or big sister. She didn't accept no for an answer from anyone, and she never accepted the excuse "I can't!" She was a very strong Christian and prayed for everyone—and that included praying for me. I knew this without her saying a word. That, I had no doubt. Although I was sure she was upset with me for not calling her back right away, she never said anything to me about it.

"Casey, Dr. Kim's nurse called and said you need to come into his office immediately. They tried paging you."

"Ruthie, I can't go right now. I have to finish with my patients, okay?"

"I already have someone coming to take your place. Go see Dr. Kim, Casey. Now!"

"Okay, Ruthie, I'm going."

Ruthie hung up the phone. I wanted to say no. I didn't want to hear what the doctor had to say. But that would have been childish. *Suck it up*, I told myself. *You're being childish.*

When I got to Dr. Kim's office, I sat in the front waiting area for maybe five minutes before his nurse called me into the back. A few minutes after that Dr. Kim came into the room with his nurse.

He shook my hand and then asked me, "How are you feeling today, Casey?"

"I'm fine, Dr. Kim."

He had the CT scan, MRI, and X-rays in his hands. "We have found the problem."

He shoved the MRI film up on the lighted screen that was hanging on the wall so he could show me what he had found. "See this, Casey?"

"Yes sir."

He was pointing to a large, round, white circle on the X-ray they had taken of my brain. "This is a tumor, Casey. It's in your left ear canal, which is behind your eardrum. It is a rather large mass, and from what I can tell, it looks like it is lying against the cerebellum part of your brain. However, part of the tumor has what looks like a hook on it. We can't tell if it has grown into your brain or not. It's in a hard position to see. This is the reason you can't hear. This is also the reason for your headaches and the dizziness you're having."

I was paralyzed with shock. I just sat there staring at the white image on the X-ray. I couldn't believe it. It was true; I had a tumor in my brain. After a few minutes had gone by, I finally got the words to come out of my mouth. They had been stuck there. I didn't want to speak them because I thought if I said them out loud, it would all be real. But I had to know; I had to know.

"Dr. Kim, am I going to die?"

He looked me straight in the eyes. "Casey, it's a big tumor. If it's not removed, it will burst, and yes, then you could die. This is serious. We don't want to wait. Let's not think about dying; let's concentrate on getting you to a doctor who can remove the tumor. I went to school with a doctor who specializes in these kinds of operations. I'm confident I can get you an appointment with him. Would you like me to give him a call and see if we can get you in?"

"Please," I said. I didn't know what else to say. I mean, what was there left to say? I felt numb.

Dr. Kim was giving his nurse some orders. I wasn't listening to them; I was still looking at the image on the wall. Then he turned back to me and began to speak to me once again.

"I want you to know that I'm here for you, Casey, if you need me. I will do whatever I can to help you. Please just call me."

The whole time Dr. Kim was talking to me I was staring at the image on the X-ray. I couldn't take my eyes off of the white dot. It was just a white circle on the X-ray film. How could that kill anyone? Once again I said to myself, *Why, Lord? Why me?*

Later that night I lay in bed crying and praying. I didn't want to die. That was funny because there were times in my life when I wished I had never been born. But now that I was faced with dying, I wanted to live. I wanted God to spare my life. I was worried about what was going to happen to me, and most importantly, what was going to happen to my children? They had no one to take care of them, at least not like I could. Their dad couldn't take care of them alone, and my mom wouldn't take them because she worked seven days a week.

Chapter 6

After a solid month of pleading with the insurance company about which doctor was going to perform my brain surgery and what hospital I would go to, the insurance company stood firm on its decision that I had to use its surgeon. It was depressing to think about dying every minute of the day and then have the added stress of not knowing what doctor was going to perform the surgery. I was getting more depressed every day. I spent day after day on the phone with the insurance company and my doctors regarding the surgery. Dr. Kim had gotten in touch with his colleague who had actually perfected a technique to remove this particular type of brain tumor. But because of the insurance company's policy, I had to use its doctor and the hospital that was in the company's network.

Even though the surgeon that Dr. Kim referred me to had perfected the surgery, the insurance company's surgeon was a five-star doctor in its network and had performed the same type of surgery before. The surgeon that Dr. Kim had recommended had even agreed to perform the surgery for free if my insurance company would pay for the hospital and the anesthesiologist. But the company wouldn't agree to that either. So I had to use its doctor.

At my first appointment with the insurance company's surgeon, Dr. Michaels explained the risks of the surgery, including paralysis and even death. However, he said. "I don't expect any complications during your surgery. I have performed this operation before, and there haven't been any complications. I have had great success performing this surgery."

He was a tall, slender man and I found him peculiar. The tone of his voice was dry and dull. His facial features were like chiseled stone. And when he talked, his eyes pierced right through me. I felt very uncomfortable when he spoke to me; I felt as if he was belittling me. He paced around the room, and at times it was like he was giving a speech to an audience and not talking to me, his patient.

"You should be back to work in about six to eight weeks," Dr. Michaels said. "You will probably spend one night in ICU for observation and your second night in a room on the nurses' floor. After that I will release you to go home. Do you have any questions?"

"No," I said, "I can't think of any."

"Good. My nurse will set up the date and time. I will see you then." He shook my hand and left the room.

After he left, I got up and walked out to the front where the nurses were. I felt empty and hopeless. I had no confidence in him, none at all. He wasn't personable like Dr. Kim or Dr. Mills, but he was my only way of getting this tumor removed from my head. There was nothing else I could do. I felt stuck.

Chapter 7

The time between finding out that I had a brain tumor and having the brain surgery was crazy. I had to stop working because the dizzy spells were happening every day. Driving became too dangerous at times. The headaches also seemed to get worse. The only way to get through the day was to lie perfectly still in a dark room with a cold rag over my eyes. That was the only thing that seemed to help the headaches and, of course, the medicines that my doctors had prescribed. The depression really had set in. I cried a lot. I found that crying and feeling sorry for myself tended to drive people away, even those who loved me. I know I lost a few good friends during that time.

Please understand me when I say I don't blame them. I didn't know what to do to help me either. So I spent a lot of that time praying and talking to God. I learned to lean on God more during that time in my life. I didn't talk to many people because I didn't know what to say to them, and the people that I did tell were in shock and didn't know what to say to me. I already had run off a few people, and I didn't need to make things worse. So I just didn't talk openly about it. I wasn't good at sharing my true feelings anyway. What do you say? "Guess what? I went to the doctor the other day and he said I have a tumor in my brain and I might die from it!" What a conversation starter, right?

I didn't let my children know what was going on. I felt they were too young, and I didn't want to scare them. However, when it came time for me to go into the hospital for surgery, I did tell them that I needed to have ear surgery. The whole time I stayed in prayer. I finally told my pastor and my prayer group what was going on, and they prayed with me. My prayer group gave me scriptures to read, and that helped a lot. It taught me to lean on my faith. They also stayed in prayer for me when I went into the hospital. I know that's what kept me from losing my mind. I hate to think how things might have been if God hadn't been in the midst! Even with people praying, I felt so exhausted and alone. The depression was bad, but prayer kept me going. I prayed for God to take care of not only me but also my children. I prayed that God would heal me completely.

Chapter 8

I had to be at the hospital by five thirty in the morning. The surgery was going to start at seven O'clock. So I staggered out of bed and into the bathroom, took my shower, and got dressed. The entire time I was showering, I was thinking about dying. It was those thoughts of dying that had kept me from falling asleep the previous night. The thoughts of dying had been nonstop since the day I saw the tumor on the X-ray screen.

After I found out that I actually had a tumor in my brain and had the X-ray in my hand, I told my ex-husband, my mother, and a few other family members about it. D. B. and my mother could no longer tell me there was nothing wrong and to suck it up. The proof was in the X-ray. D. B. offered to drive me to the hospital. On the way we didn't speak much; we just got into the car and headed twenty or so miles to the hospital. Every once in a while he would say, "Are you okay? You do know you're going to be fine." I remember looking at him and wondering why we couldn't just talk to each other like this without tearing each other apart. God didn't want people to act like that toward each other. God said to love one another. So why did we have to constantly fight with each other? God wanted us to do all things with love and understanding. Why couldn't we just be civil to each other? Now that I was dying, nothing seemed important anymore, not so important that we would have to fight over it. I was all alone. How? When? Why did this happen to me? I didn't want to be alone. I was terrified.

I had sent our children to a friend's house for a few days, at least until I came back home from the hospital. I told my friend I was going to have ear surgery and that I would be back home in just a few days. I said not to worry about me; I was going to be fine but to please keep me in her prayers.

I remember looking out of the car window as we drove into the hospital parking lot; it was so dark. It looked eerie. It was as if I was the only person in the world. I was carrying the weight of the world on my shoulders, and the fate of my children lay heavily on my mind. The feeling of being alone was almost overwhelming. No one was there for me, no one! I was going to die alone. I remember asking God not to let me die alone. No one cared, not even my mother. She told D. B. to call her if something happened to me during the surgery. Can you believe it? My own mother. She wasn't going to be there for me. I really didn't expect her to be anyway. She hated the way I lived my life. And she couldn't stand to be in the same room with D. B. She said he scared her and she didn't like being around him. My mom never was there emotionally for me. I don't think she knew how to be emotionally connected to anyone. My dad blamed her lack of emotions on her hard childhood. I think she was scared of being hurt so she chose not to show any emotion. But that's another story for another time. I will say this: God can change anyone; he changed her before she passed away.

I could die, and no one cared. Nobody. Not even the people who said they loved me.

As we entered the hospital lobby, my mind was racing with thoughts of death and dying. Where would I go, heaven or hell? If I died, surely I'd go to heaven. God does forgive people who ask for his forgiveness, right? I had accepted Jesus Christ a long time ago as my Savior, and I knew he had died for my sins. I knew this to be the truth. I had been in church all my life, and I had read the Bible many times. So I should have known without a doubt that God was in total control.

But then fear crept into my mind, and of course, doubt started to sneak in. Then that little voice in the back of my mind said, "You know you haven't lived a Christian life, not the kind of life God wants you to live. You have broken God's commandments.

God knows every one of your sins. He knows everything! God's not going to let you into heaven. You're a sinner!"

I wasn't proud of the fact that I hadn't lived as I should have. And it was true: I had broken most of God's commandments; I had broken some of them repeatedly. Could God really forgive a person like me? I had read the Bible, but as I said I hadn't lived a Christian life. I went to church; in fact just about every time the church doors were open, I was there. I even helped at the church. But I knew I wasn't the person God intended me to be. This worried me.

I was so scared. I could feel my body shaking. I didn't want to parish in hell for eternity. I remember praying and asking God to forgive me. It was more like begging God. I prayed, "Lord, if this is the end of my life, I want to go to heaven and be with you. Please remember me, Lord."

I walked up to the front desk and the receptionist told us that a nurse from surgery would come for me and to have a seat in the waiting room. It was so cold in the hospital. I remember wishing I had brought a sweater with me. I was already shaking from the thoughts of dying; now I was cold to go along with it.

It wasn't long before the nurse came and took us to a room in the back. She explained that this was where I would wait until someone took me to surgery. Soon the surgical nurse came into the room. She introduced herself and told me she would be with me during my operation. She said that she would come back and start an IV in my arm. The doctor needed the IV to administer medicines during surgery. She also told me that she was going to give me something to help me relax. She talked with me for a few minutes about what to expect when I came out of surgery. Then she left to get the medicine.

When the surgical nurse returned a short time later, she was with the anesthesiologist. He introduced himself and asked me a couple of questions, including if I was allergic to any medicines and if I had eaten or had anything to drink. He didn't stay but a few seconds. As he was leaving, he looked back at me with a smile and said, "I'll see you in the back; it won't be much longer."

The nurse gave me the shot to help me relax. It wasn't long after the shot that they came and wheeled me into surgery. I remember saying good-bye to my ex-husband and staring at the lights as they wheeled me down the hall into the operating room. (When I think about saying that last good-bye, I realized that it was almost a forever good-bye!)

Chapter 9

The next thing I knew I was being placed on a golden staircase. One part of the staircase went straight up toward heaven. But halfway up the staircase it split into two. One part of the staircase veered off to the right. I didn't know where that staircase led to, but I knew I didn't want to be on it.

At first I was scared. I didn't realize I was on the staircase to heaven; however, I continued to travel upward. The farther I traveled, the more I became aware of where I was and that an angel had carried me there and set me down on the staircase. The farther I climbed, the more my fear subsided. I was no longer scared. In fact, I had a peaceful feeling. It was quiet and beautiful. It was like nothing I had ever experienced.

There was a blue sky that looked like thousands of drops of liquid crystals. The greens were the deepest, darkest emeralds you would ever see. However, there was one thing that stood out from everything else. It was the fragrance that filled the air. I had never smelled anything so wonderful in all my life. That fragrance sticks with me to this very day. I have searched for something that smells similar, but I haven't found anything close to it. At the time, I questioned what that smell was. Later on, my aunt would show me in the Bible where it talked about a sweet aroma. The aroma that I smelled in heaven had the sweetest, cleanest, purest, scent imaginable like an expensive perfume. I can only begin to describe it to you. But I will say this, it was not of this world.

I knew one thing for certain: "God is here," I said. I could feel his presence. I couldn't see him, but my spirit knew he was there. A joy began to fill my soul, a wonderful happiness. I hadn't felt such happiness, not in my lifetime!

At the top of the stairs, standing on the balcony, I could see shapes of people. I felt as if I knew them, but I couldn't see their faces so I wasn't sure. I could hear them saying something, but I couldn't understand them. Who were these people? That's when I realized I must have died. How else would I have gotten here?

Near the top of the staircase I saw my dad. He was walking down the staircase toward me. This had to be the happiest I had been since he had died. My dad had passed away many years ago. He was killed when a train struck his truck as he was crossing a railroad track while he was working. I started running up the staircase to give my dad a hug. I loved and missed him so much.

There hadn't been a day that went by that I didn't think about him. My dad was my world. We were very close when I was a young girl. However, there were things that happened between us when I was a teenager that put a strain on our relationship. I had fallen in love with someone he didn't approve of, and with good reason. Being young, I wouldn't listen to my dad. I would regret this decision later on in my life. I never got to tell him I was sorry or how much I loved him and that he had been right. The guilt would eat at me for years. My mother blamed me for my dad's death. That always stuck in the back of my mind. I didn't understand why she blamed me, but in her mind his death was my fault. Now he was walking down to me, and he looked so good.

Dad looked young and healthy, dressed in his tan khaki pants and brown T-shirt. For some reason he was dressed as if he were going to work. When I reached him, I started to give him a hug, but he put his hands up and stopped me from touching him. He then began to speak to me. "Daughter, you can't touch me. You have to go back to be with your mother and brother. You can't stay here with me. God said you have to go back." This still brings me to tears every time I think about not being able to stay in heaven, about my dad telling me I couldn't stay with him in heaven. It hurts.

The whole time he was speaking to me he had his hands up in front of him. "You have to go back now," he said. I couldn't believe my dad was telling me I couldn't stay with him. Why did I have to leave? "Why can't I just stay here with you, Dad? Please?" I asked. But he didn't answer me. He just kept telling me to go back, and I kept asking him why.

"Dad, why are you dressed like you're going to work?"

"I'm working on the new world that God is preparing for us," he said. "You have to go back now and tell everyone what you have seen and heard."

But I kept begging him. "Please don't make me go back, Dad, please! I hate it there. I'm all alone there. Nobody cares about me. It's horrible, Dad. I miss you so much. Don't you want me to stay with you? Please?"

I remember telling him, "I'll just hold my breath, and then I won't have to go back down there. I'll die for sure." The last thing I remember my dad saying to me was "Child, don't you know God is in control of the very breath that you breathe?"

Then, in a split second, it was all gone. Everything! My dad, the staircase, and the wonderful fragrance! They were all gone, and I was alone once again.

I realized I wasn't standing on the staircase anymore. I was in my ex-mother-in-law's bathroom, and I was standing behind her.

She was looking in the mirror, fixing her hair, and talking to God. I could hear her and see exactly what she was doing. She looked so sad. Her eyes were filled with tears. I didn't want her to be sad, and for some reason I had such compassion for her. I wanted her to stop crying. Everything was going to be all right. God had sent me back. I didn't get to stay in heaven.

Later on, when I had the opportunity to talk to my ex-mother-in-law about what happened when I died, I told her what I had seen and heard. I described to her what she was doing and what she was wearing; I told her that as she was talking with God and holding on to a silver chain around her neck. I asked her about the chain. She explained to me that the chain had once held a cross on it, that her son had given it to her, and that it held a very special place in her heart. I told her that I had heard her calling me by my nickname, that she was crying and telling me to hang on. I told her that I saw and heard her praying to God. I told her that she had asked God to save me and let me live. I was trying to tell her that I was okay and that I was alive. I tried to let her know that I didn't get to stay in heaven. I was sent back. I remember trying to comfort her and said, "I'm standing right here behind you; I'm okay." But she couldn't see or hear me. That's how I know that our loved ones who have passed on watch over us because I could see and hear my family. I could see them and I could hear them, but no matter what I said or did, they couldn't hear or see me.

Again, in an instance, I was in the backseat of my brother's car. Somehow I knew that my brother was driving to the hospital to see me. My mother was sitting on the passenger side. She had her hand on his knee, squeezing it tightly and crying. My sister-in-law, Macy, who is my brother's wife, was in the backseat, sitting behind my mother. I was sitting next to her. I could see them clearly, but they couldn't see me. I also knew my brother was driving too fast and needed to slow down. He was going seventy-one miles per hour. I kept telling him to slow down. "Please, Bubba, slow down. I'm okay." But he couldn't hear me. Even when I yelled at him, he couldn't hear me. No one knew I had been sent back.

Then I felt it, the cold air going into my lungs. My dad was right: God is in control of our every breath!

Chapter 10

Days later I would wake up, disappointed and depressed. I still cry at times when I think about how I had to leave heaven and come back here. I will never forget what I saw and heard the day I died and went to heaven. It has forever changed my life. But I have learned to accept the fact that I was sent back. I can't change anything but me. Of course I'm just human, and I still get down in the dumps at times. And for a long time, all I thought about was dying so I could get back to heaven and to that wonderful aroma. I had a hard time accepting that I had to come back down here. What possible reason could I have to come back down here? Well, I now know one of the reasons was to write this book. It's not my will, but God's will, and everything is in accordance to his will. But when I smell that fragrance, I'll know I'm back in the presence of my God, and I'll also know that my dad's not too far away. Oh, what a glorious day that will be.

When I opened my eyes for the first time after the brain surgery, I saw my two sons and a close friend of theirs kneeling at my bedside, with their heads bowed, their eyes closed, and their hands clasped together. I knew they were praying for me. When they looked up at me, I could see the tears running down their faces. My precious babies—even they knew to talk to God. They had enough faith in God to know that he would make everything all right.

My mother, my brother, and his wife, Macy, stood behind my boys. I remember thinking this was odd because I just had been in the backseat of my brother's car. Now they were looking down at me lying in this hospital bed.

Standing on the other side of my bed were some of my other family members—a couple of aunts, Honey and Louise—and even my ex-mother-in-law. (*She's here?* I thought to myself. *I was just at her house.*) Standing beside her was one of her daughters, Sandy. At the foot of my bed was Uncle Dale, and beside him was a very close friend of mine from school, Nicky. I had seen her in town just a few days before my surgery. I had told her about it and asked if she would please come to the hospital on the day of my surgery and be there for me. She said she would. It made me feel so good to see her there. She had kept her promise to me, and that was worth more than anything in this world.

They were all trying to talk to me, and they were asking me questions. Much of what they were saying, however, didn't make any sense to me, but at least they were there for me. I wasn't alone anymore. I wanted to tell them that I had gone to heaven and saw my dad. I wanted them to know that heaven did exist and that God was preparing a new world for us. God is coming back for us. It's all true.

I really wanted to let my mom know that I had seen and talked to my dad and that he was fine. He was up in heaven with God. But I was unable to speak. I had tubes in my mouth and my nose. There was something pushing on the bottoms on my feet. (Later on I found out that it was a machine that keeps blood clots, which could go to your heart, from forming in your legs.) My head hurt and only one of my eyes would open. I just wanted to go to sleep. I was so tired. Then I started crying. Everyone assumed it was because I was in pain. They called for the nurse to get me something for pain, but the truth was that I was crying because I didn't get to stay in heaven. That's where I wanted to be.

Days later I would wake up again. I would find out that my brain had swollen and I had died for the second time. They had to rush me back into surgery to relieve the pressure on my brain. The nurses told me that the doctor had to open up the top of my skull to relieve the pressure.

In my Father's Land

The doctor told me that when he was performing the surgery, he had accidentally cut the primary motor cortex of my brain (it controls voluntary movement). My brain had swollen because of a dysfunctional drain tube that had been placed at the base of my brain during surgery. It was supposed to drain the excess fluids off of my brain and down into my stomach, but for some reason the tube didn't drain properly. The only way for the swelling to go down was for the doctor to take me back into surgery and relieve the pressure on my brain by cutting open my skull and draining the excess brain fluid. Then he had to wait and see how I would do.

Dr. Michaels had left for vacation, and the only doctor the nurses could get to perform the procedure on such short notice was the ER doctor. He hadn't performed this type of surgery before, but there wasn't any time to waste. I wasn't breathing and something had to be done *stat*!

A few days after my second brain surgery, the ER doctor came into the ICU and tried to explain to me what had happened while he was performing the surgery and why it happened. He kept apologizing to me for cutting my brain. To tell you the truth, I never held anything against him; he was trying to save my life. I admired him for doing what he could for me. In fact this same doctor would come to my rescue again a few days later. This just goes to show that we all have a purpose in life and that God uses us to help one another. I believe God used the ER doctor to save my life not once but twice! God bless those who choose to listen to God's voice.

A couple of days later, for no apparent reason, the left side of my chest collapsed and began to hurt. I couldn't breathe, and the pain was intense. I began to panic. The alarm on my bed began to go off. A nurse came running up to my bedside.

"Are you okay? What's wrong?" she asked me.

I couldn't speak to tell her that I couldn't breathe. Thank God she could see I was scared and that my breathing was in distress. Within seconds another nurse came to see what was going on.

"What's wrong?" she asked the first nurse.

"Call the ER doctor *stat*."

The ER doctor was there in an instance. It was the same young doctor from a few days earlier who had removed the fluid from my brain. His examination was quick. He told the nurse that I had a pneumothorax (a collapsed lung). He told her what he was going to need, and then he turned his attention back to me. He began to explain to me what was happening to my breathing. He told me that my left lung had collapsed.

"This is what I'm going to do so you will be able to breathe," he said.

In my Father's Land

As he was talking to me, the nurse arrived with the tray of items he had requested. "I'm going to turn you onto your right side," he explained as he began to move me onto my side. He then took my left arm and put it over my head.

"Now," he said, "I'm going to make a small incision between your ribs. It's going to hurt, but I can't give you anything for pain right now, okay? I need you to lie perfectly still. Please don't move. After I make the incision, I'm going to put a tube into your lung. You will feel the air going into your lung, and then you will be able to breathe. It won't take long. It will be over soon."

As he was talking, I felt the pain of the knife cutting into my side and the tube being pushed into my lung. It was so hard not to move; the pain was excruciating. Then I felt the air going into my left lung. The pain and the panic started to subside.

When he was done and saw that I was breathing better, he reassured me. "The tube can come out in a few days, okay? You're going to be fine now."

He patted me on my shoulder and said, "Good job, hang in there. I'll come back and check in on you later."

He came back later that afternoon to see how I was doing. He would come to check on me often, just about every time he worked. Finally the day came when the tube was going to be removed from my lung. I was so glad because it hurt, and it was hard to sleep with it because I was always hitting it with my arm.

When the doctor came walking in, he was smiling, "Well," he said, "are you ready to get that tube out? Hopefully your lung is strong enough to work on its own by now. Let's see how it looks."

Once again he rolled me onto my right side, with my left arm stretched up over my head, and he began to take the tube out of my lung. But something went wrong; I couldn't breathe and the pain was horrible. He told me, "I'm going to need to leave the tube in for a little bit longer. Your lung isn't strong enough yet. It's trying to collapse again. I'm sorry, but we can try again in a few days. For now we need to leave it in."

A couple of days went by, and he came back and tried again to remove the tube. This time it was a success, I was breathing on my own. Thanks to God!

Because of the ER doctor and other people like him, I have been led to believe that God puts certain people into our lives. These people have a great purpose in our lives. We might not ever know why God has chosen these people, but that is between them and God. Your job is to be thankful that God loves you enough to send them.

Chapter 11

Days came and went, and I slept most of the time. Keeping up with what day it was and the time of day really didn't matter to me anymore. Nothing mattered to me anymore.

Every day my ex-husband came to the hospital and fed me at lunchtime. It would take him hours to get me to eat half of the food on my tray. Like I said, God sends people to you when you need them. A friend told me that I wouldn't eat for anyone else but him. I always thought that was odd, but he had the patience to stay there and feed me. I couldn't feed myself. My head and hands shook uncontrollably. I couldn't hold on to silverware or a glass; I had to drink through a straw while someone held the glass. Someone had to help me, and thank God my ex was kind enough to do the job. I was told that he came every day and sometimes even at night. If you knew about our relationship and all the horrors of it, you would realize that just coming to help me eat was an act of kindness. Only God could get him to do something so caring. That was truly a blessing.

My friend Nicky visited me just about every day. She would come during visitation hours, and when I got into my own room, she would stay overnight with me. It was always good to see her standing at my bedside, smiling down at me. I guess she gave me hope that things would get better. Nicky always made me laugh, and she also knew how to pray! It was always comforting to me when she prayed over me.

The nurses came by my bedside and checked on me every few minutes, changing the IV bags or taking my vital signs. Whatever I needed at the time, the nurses were there. They always spoke to me, even when I couldn't speak to them. They kept me informed about everything that was going on with my health. They reassured me that they were close by if I needed them. They tried to make me comfortable and suggested that I get some rest so I could regain my strength. They told me who had called to check in on me or if someone had come to visit me while I was sleeping. Of course I slept a lot. The nurses always spoke about how my aunt Honey came in before the surgery and prayed over everything, including the bed and the curtain, and of course she prayed for them. They smiled and told me how blessed I was to be alive and doing so well, that I had died not just once but twice. "God has his hands on you," the nurses said. Most of them had never known a person who died and came back from heaven. "You're truly blessed," they said. The problem was I didn't feel very blessed at the time. I was depressed. I didn't get to stay in heaven.

The day finally came when the nurse was going to take out all the tubes, including my catheter. I was going to be tube-free. That was a big day, according to them. It was a step forward in my recovery process. A nurse had removed the feeding tube weeks ago so I could eat solid foods. I just didn't feel like eating. The nose cannula had been in since surgery, and it hurt when it was removed. I have a scar on my nose from where it had rubbed a sore on it. The scar is a reminder of the day they removed the tubes.

After the nurse had removed the tubes, she told me, "If your vital signs stay stable, we can move you into a private room. It will still be on the ICU floor, but, Casey, you will be in your own room. Your family and friends can come see you any time they want to; there are no visiting hours."

After the nurse left, I started crying. I was glad to be going into my own room. It meant that the doctors and nurses thought I was getting better. Every day was a challenge, but this meant I was making progress. Then, as always, my thoughts went straight to my children. Maybe they would get to come to the hospital and visit me. I wondered all the time what they were doing and if they missed me as much as I missed them. And of course I prayed. I talked to God a lot when I was lying in that hospital bed.

The next day they moved me into a private room. It was across from the nurses' station so they could still keep an eye on me. My friend Nicky came to stay with me as often as she could, and D. B. still came every day to give me my lunch. But eating just wasn't something I cared to do. My mother came sometimes. I had other visitors as well, but I can't remember who came or who called. I was still sleeping a lot. It was nice when Nicky came to spend the night with me. She hadn't changed a bit from when I knew her in school. She was such a sweet and caring person. I told Nicky everything that I saw and heard, and about the wonderful aroma in heaven. I would never forget that fragrance.

"Nicky," I said, "I knew that God was there with me. I never saw him, but I could feel his presence. And, Nicky, I saw my dad."

"You never saw God?" Nicky asked.

"No, but I knew he was there."

I told her about the colors and the staircase and about the people on the balcony. I knew they were our loved ones who had passed on and people we had known throughout our lives. "But I couldn't see their faces," I told her. I explained how disappointed and hurt I was that I had to come back. She sat for hours brushing out the tangles from my matted hair—what little hair I had left on my head—and listened to me ramble on and on for hours about heaven.

"Sister," she said, "you scared me to death. When that doctor came out and told us that you had died during surgery, and he told me and your mother that they had to resuscitate you, I almost passed out right there. I just couldn't believe it!

"And then he explained how he had to remove a large portion of your skull and replace it with a type of wax, and that you would be in ICU for a very long time. Dr. Michaels said, 'Only time will tell how she is going to do.'"

Nicky told me how my mother got angry and said, "I can't believe she would pull something like this. I knew this was going to happen." Nicky said that when she turned around, my mother was leaving. Nicky asked my mother, "Are you leaving her?" And my mother replied, "Yes, she is getting what she deserves." Nicky said to her, "I can't believe you're going to leave your daughter up here like this. She just had brain surgery and died." But my mother just turned and walked away.

When I first heard how my mother reacted, it hurt me so badly. I had to pray and ask God to help me find a way to forgive her. I will always wonder why my mother said those things. How could she have been so angry at me? And why? I would have never blamed someone for dying, and I certainly wouldn't have just gotten up and left someone that I loved. I needed her. But shock can cause us to act in a way we don't normally act.

After my mother had left, Nicky asked the doctor when she could see me. He told her that she would be able to see me in a few minutes, and he would send a nurse to get her. The nurse would bring Nicky into the recovery room so she could sit with me for a few minutes. Not long after the doctor left, a nurse led her into the room where I was lying. As the nurse opened the door, Nicky couldn't believe what she was seeing. I was laid out on the bed with tubes in me.

"You looked horrible," Nicky said, "but thank God they brought you back!"

A nurse was standing at my bedside. She looked over at Nicky and the nurse as they walked through the door and said, "God's not finished with this one yet; she's back."

Nicky said, "All I could do was cry and praise God."

Later Nicky told me, "Me and you had a long talk while you was laying there!" Funny thing is she never told me what she talked about. However, she did say that at one point she told me, "Casey, if you can hear me, squeeze my hand." Nicky said, "I felt you squeeze my hand very lightly. I knew you heard me then and that you were going to be okay."

In my Father's Land

Nicky and I were both crying as she told the story of what happened on the day of my surgery. I think I cried because it made me think about my dad telling me I couldn't stay and that I had to leave heaven and come back down here. I think Nicky cried because God had created a miracle, and she had been a witness to his marvelous works.

Chapter 12

The nurses who had taken care of me during and after the surgery came to visit me in my room every day, and so did the young ER doctor who had saved my life twice. I guess since I had been in the hospital for close to a month, they had gotten used to taking care of me. They told me it was a miracle that I was still there with them. Every one of the nurses helped me. They tried to keep my spirits up. Every day they tried to encourage me to walk and to try to feed myself. But my brain just wasn't working like it had before. The more I tried to do things, the more frustrated I became. When I got frustrated, depression set in.

My thought process was so slow that I couldn't relate to most people. I knew that my mind wasn't right, but I didn't know what to do about it. So I prayed for God to have mercy on me. Life was hard, very hard. I tried to walk but I would fall, so I had to use a wheelchair. I remembered how much I loved my stiletto heels and that I wanted to walk in them again. I still needed help eating.

No matter how hard I tried, I still couldn't hold a glass or my silverware. Because my hands and my head shook uncontrollably, I just lay with my head on my pillow; that was the only way I could keep it from shaking. I was so embarrassed. I had gained so much weight even though I wasn't eating a lot. All of this sent me into a deep depression.

The old me was gone, and I didn't know if I would ever come back. I think that was the worst thing, knowing my mind was gone, knowing I would never be the same. My hopes and dreams were shattered. I would never drive again. Work was something in the past. What was I going to do? Why did this have to happen to me? Why God? Please help me.

Dr. Michaels came into my room one afternoon to talk to me about being released. "Casey," he said, "I need you to try to walk, and I also need you to try to eat. I spoke with your mother about you being released from the hospital. I asked her where you would be going. Your mother told me that she couldn't take care of you. She doesn't have the time to take care of you because she works seven days a week. She thought it would be best for me to send you to a nursing home where you would get the proper care. Casey, you will need someone to help you with personal care as well as your medicines. I really don't want to send you to a nursing home, but

I don't know of any other place you could go. You have to try to walk and feed yourself."

At that moment it was like my life was over. I was going to a nursing home. My family was throwing me away! This is what I was sent back from heaven for? Please, God! Please take me back to heaven. For the next couple of days, I tried to walk and feed myself. It was horrible. Every time I tried to walk I fell, so the nurses would put me into a wheelchair. They wouldn't give up on me, even when I wanted to give up on myself. Every few hours they came with a walker and I attempted to walk again. This went on for weeks. I was tired, and it hurt to walk. Trying to feed myself was embarrassing. I spilled the food all over me, the bed, and the floor. Since I couldn't walk, I wasn't able to go to the bathroom when I needed to go, and I had to use a bed pan. That meant I had to call for the nurse, and I hated to do that. I hated asking for help. The nurses also had to give me a bed bath because I couldn't stand up in the shower. I couldn't do anything for myself; I was totally dependent on the nurses.

I felt useless. I cried and asked God why I had to come back. I must have asked God why every day. I would be better off dead. I begged God to let me die. The doctor came by to check on my progress just about every day. He tried to encourage me. He didn't want to send me to a nursing home, but if I couldn't walk or feed myself, he would have no choice but to put me where someone could take care of me.

The doctor came in one afternoon and told me he was going to release me the following day. My first thought was that I was going to a nursing home and my life was over. But he told me that I was going home. I thought my mother had a change of heart and was going to take care of me. It wasn't till the next day that I found out I was going to go to my ex-husband's home. After being in the hospital for what seemed like a lifetime, I was finally leaving! My ex-husband came into my room and told me he was there to take me home. I was grateful to him because I knew the alternative was a nursing home. At least at his house I could be with my children. I missed them so much. They were the only reason I had to live. I had taken a few steps with a walker; however, I shuffled my feet when I walked. My feet wouldn't do what I wanted them to do, and I was so weak. This made me still dependent on the wheelchair.

The doctors recommended physical therapy and for a home health agency to come out to my ex's house. The home health nurse would help with my bathing and my medicines. The physical therapist would help me regain the strength in my arms and legs. However, I never saw either one of them until I got into my own apartment. The ride home was tiring and painful. My head hurt and my legs cramped terribly. It did feel somewhat good to get out of the hospital though. When we arrived home, it took a long time for me to get into the house. I had gained a significant amount of weight, and it was hard for me to move. My legs wouldn't work, and I was out of breath. The hospital had given me a walker to use, but that didn't really help much. I felt so weak. And I was very frustrated. I just wanted to die.

Living with my ex-husband in his house was hard. I had been in the hospital for more than a month and everything about me had changed, including my looks. I went into the hospital at 145 pounds; now I weighed 335 pounds. I needed a lot of care. The fact that my ex-husband and I had different lifestyles added to the tension. He loved the nightlife and party life; I liked to hang around the house. We couldn't agree on anything, and we argued constantly. I didn't want to argue; I just wanted to be well! However, I wasn't in a nursing home and I was able to be with my children, so I was going to try and overlook the things he said or did. I was grateful for one thing: he had brought me there. He left me home alone most nights while he went out on the town, so it was up to my daughter, Amy, to do what she could to help me. My oldest son was nineteen and had moved in with his grandmother. My middle son, who was seventeen at the time, stayed pretty busy. When he wasn't in school, he spent most of his time at his girlfriend's house down the road. Amy, who was the baby, was only six years old when all this happened.

One afternoon it was time for my bath. D. B. put me into my wheelchair and wheeled me into the bathroom. With my bath water in the tub and clean clothes sitting by the sink, I was ready for my bath. D. B. helped me into the bathtub as he had done so many times before, but this time was going to be different. After I had washed up, I yelled for him to come and help get out of the bathtub. At first he didn't answer me. Then, after a few minutes, I heard D. B. say, "Casey, if you want out of the bathtub, get yourself out. You can do it; just try!"

I can't tell you how long I was in the bathtub. I had no comprehension of time. But I know that I was really cold and my skin was wrinkled and splotched. I cried and screamed for him to come and help me, but he never came. I was so scared. I was left there all alone. After a while I was able to pick up my right leg and throw it over the bathtub. Then I used my arms to pull the rest of my body over the side of the tub so I could fall onto the floor. After I fell onto the bathroom floor, I was able to reach for my towel to dry off and cover up myself. I eventually was able to pull myself onto the toilet, and I sat there for a while.

At some point I remember looking up at the door. It was cracked open. That's when I saw my walker. My wheelchair had been replaced with my walker. I knew at that point I had to learn how to walk again. D. B. wasn't going to help me; I was on my own. No one could do it for me; I had to do this for myself. No one was going to help me but me! After I dressed myself, I managed to get to the walker. Slowly I made it into the living room where D. B. had been sitting on the couch the whole time. As I came around the corner, he looked up at me and smiled.

"I knew you could do it," D. B. said. "You're stronger than you think, Casey. You have to help yourself; no one can do it for you."

When I look back at that moment, I realize that was one of the greatest days of my recovery because that was the day I started walking.

It's sad, but my daughter, Amy, grew up before it was her time. Because I had seizures often, she had to climb up onto a dining room chair and call 911. She had memorized our address and phone number to give to the 911 operator. And when the paramedics came, Amy talked to them. She knew what to tell them and could even give them my medications. She was just a little six-year-old girl taking care of her very sick mommy. This always made me sad. I was supposed to be taking care of her.

Chapter 13

Finally the day came. After living in D. B.'s home for a little over six months, Amy and I were ready to move into our own apartment. It was just a few doors from where my middle son, Hank, lived, so if I ever needed anything, he was close by. I was able to walk a lot better and do some things like cook and clean the house. I was so glad to get into our own place and out of D. B.'s house. Now he could live his life and I could live mine.

It was a struggle being on our own. I had little money, and I couldn't work to make any extra money. But we made it, thanks to God; he always made sure we had food to eat and a roof over our head. I know it was harder on Amy than it was for me. She didn't have what most other children had, and she always was worried about me. Most of the time we depended on other people's kindness to help us. The money I got every month from my disability check went toward the rent and bills. We got assistance with food but very little. The only way we made it was by the grace of God. It broke my heart when I couldn't buy Amy something from the corner store. Most children asked for candy or a toy when they went into the store with a parent, but not Amy, not since I came home from the hospital. Somehow she understood that we couldn't afford it.

Over the next few years Amy and I moved many times. That poor little baby girl switched from one school to another. But again God is great, and he always saw us through. We never knew where we were going to live from one month to the next, but four years after my surgery, Amy and I moved to the neighboring state of Louisiana. I wanted to get away from everything and everybody, so I thought this would be a great way to do just that. By moving to a different state, we could have a brand-new start. But things were hard for the first six months, and it came to a point when there was hardly any food to eat. Every day we ate an egg with toast for breakfast, and at night we shared a sandwich and, if we had them, a few chips. At least Amy was able to eat one good meal a day. Every penny I got went to the rent and lights, so there was no extra money for anything else—not for food or clothes, nothing!

Kathy, a cousin of my ex-husband, came to check on us. Her daughter, Annie, had come to our house and saw that we didn't have enough to eat and that Amy was walking to school in the cold without a coat. Annie went straight home and told her mom about our situation. Kathy came to see for herself what was going on, and when she came in, she said that she knew we were struggling. She said that she had peeked into the refrigerator and saw it was empty. She wanted us to come and stay with her and her husband, Will, and their children. I didn't know what to say; I was just so grateful that she would offer her home to us. When we finally moved into Kathy and Will's home, I knew they would never let Amy go without. For once she would have a stable life. She would have food and clothes and a coat to wear to school. She deserved so much more than what she was getting from me. Amy never knew what was going to happen from one minute to the next. I was always sick and needed to see a doctor.

We lived with Kathy and Will for a little over nine years. Kathy and I became very close friends. She was not only my friend but she also was like the sister I had always wanted. She also became my nurse. She made sure I got the help I needed. Kathy talked to her family physician and asked him if he would accept me as a new patient. He did, and in turn he referred me to a neurologist and a psychiatrist. The psychiatrist referred me to a therapist. I was finally getting the medical help I needed. I felt like I was on the road to recovery, but there were setbacks. At times instead of getting better I would get sick, really sick.

There was a time when I became so ill that the doctors told Kathy they had done all they could do for me. The neurologist explained that my brain was full of holes; they referred to my brain as being "dumb punched." Nothing can be done to heal a brain that has had so much trauma and scarring. And when the doctor removed the tumor, because of its size and location, he also had to remove a large portion of my cerebellum. That caused me to having grand mal seizures daily, and they were occurring one after another. The headaches had become so painful that they were crippling. I was back to needing help with bathing, and even walking at times. The doctors gave me morphine and Demerol for pain on top of the many other medications I was already taking. But nothing stopped the seizures.

I was in and out of the hospital several times a week because of the seizures and the headaches. My doctor told Kathy, "I have done all I can for her. I don't know what else to do. Take her home and try to make her as comfortable as possible." He also told her that when I got closer to the end of my time, he would call in hospice. Kathy stayed by my side and took care of me. She never gave up on me, and she wouldn't let me give up on myself. She got me up every day as if everything was okay and I was going to get better. Needless to say she was right; I'm still here and doing quite well. I believe that is because of all the prayers Kathy and my family and friends prayed over me—and all the love and care that Kathy and her family gave me.

After nine and a half years living with Kathy and her family, I moved out on my own again. I was doing much better and getting back to a somewhat normal life. Amy had moved in with her uncle in Texas a couple of months before I moved out of Kathy and Will's house. She also was doing quite well. It was a bittersweet time in my life. Kathy always had been there to help me if I needed something, so being on my own meant I would have to depend upon myself for most everything.

My friend Nicky lived in Texas, and I decided that I would move back there. She lived in an apartment building, and there was an apartment right behind her for rent. She would be able to come by and check on me after work to make sure I had eaten and taken my medicines. Nicky took me everywhere I needed to go. We stayed busy going to resale shops and trying the new restaurants in our area. And there was always things going on at church. Nicky and I had a lot of fun hanging out together. Amy came back to live with me a couple of weeks after I moved back to Texas. She was in high school by now and was very busy with school and a new boyfriend. She was a happy teenager. Things were really going well for us.

Eventually Amy and I moved from our small hometown to Houston, Texas. Things were going great for a while, but then my medications stopped working. This caused me to have a nervous breakdown. The headaches started again and so did the seizures. The doctors put me into the hospital to adjust my medication. But once again the medicines they gave me weren't working like they should have, and the depression set back in. The doctors decided to release me to a private group therapy facility. I spent my days at the Ranch and went to a group home at night.

Chapter 14

These past five years have actually been pretty amazing. Five years ago I was living in an apartment on the outskirts of Houston, Texas, with my new friend, Phoenix. Amy was living with family friends nearby. Phoenix and I had met at the group home in downtown Houston. We became inseparable from the moment we met. We were both attending group therapy at the Ranch, located on the outskirts of Houston, for different reasons, but we both fought depression. I can tell you this: without Phoenix, I would have lost my mind. I questioned my sanity every day while I was living in the group home. That place had a way of getting you down. But Phoenix helped me to overcome my insecurities. We became such close friends; no matter what happened, we had each other's back. She reassured me that I wasn't the crazy one. I will forever be grateful to her for that. She listened to me, and she believed in me. She is truly my BFF (best friend forever).

While I was living with Phoenix, I got a call from Annie that my friend Kathy had passed away. That was such horrible news. I had just talked to her a couple of days earlier. After I heard the news of Kathy's death, I constantly called to check in on Will and their children. Will and Kathy had been high school sweethearts, and they got married right out of high school. He loved her with all his heart.

I knew this was going to devastate him, and I was worried about him. Actually I was worried he would become depressed and might hurt himself. So I called him often. We talked about everything—his work, his mom, and his brother, who had passed away on the same day. His brother and his wife passed away just four hours apart. But mostly we talked about Kathy and their children. Sometimes we would stay on the phone for hours at a time. I never really thought about how much we talked because, when I lived at their house, Kathy, Will, and I would sit at the kitchen table and talk for hours. So it wasn't anything out of the ordinary.

It wasn't until the third time Will came to visit Phoenix and me that I realized something was different between us. We greeted each other at the door with a hug, but it wasn't an ordinary hug. I had never felt anything like that in my life. I knew that I had feelings for Will from that moment on. I never thought about falling in love again. I just didn't think love was going to happen to me again. I always thought, *Who would want to be with someone who is as sick as I am?* Besides, I had told God a long time ago that I was going to wait for him to find a godly man for me. Can you believe a hug got me? Yes, I knew from hugging him that I was in love! I didn't want to let him go. For the first time in my life I felt safe.

And if God put this man in my life, everything was going to be fine. I was going to trust God. So whatever God had in store for me, so be it. I was still sick; in fact I was always sick. I was going back and forth to the hospital and taking twenty-eight pills a day. I had at least two doctor's appointments a week. That was a lot to comprehend for one person. There was a lot of stuff to deal with when you had a sick person as a girlfriend.

But when God puts two people together, everything works out. Will is a God-fearing Christian man. He is respected not only by me but also by his family and friends. His faith in God is unshakeable, and his understanding of God's word is remarkable. Not only is he a Christian man but he also walks by faith. God truly blessed me when he put Will in my life.

Chapter 15

The apartment I shared with Phoenix was a hundred miles from where Will lived and worked, so on October first, I moved back to Louisiana to be closer to him. We decided in order to pursue a relationship one of us would have to move, and since his work was in Louisiana, it would be easier for me to move to his home state of Louisiana. He already knew I took a lot of medications; in fact we had talked about how I hated taking all the pills and that my hope was to one day be free from medication. However, I knew that would only happen with God's healing touch. Only through his mercy and by his grace would I be healed.

Once I moved to Louisiana, Will began to research all the medications I was taking. He found that several of them were counteracting each other. He also learned that some of them could actually be causing me to have the seizures and that in turn would cause the headaches.

If Will wasn't on the computer researching my medications, he was talking to someone about finding a new doctor for me, a doctor close to where we lived. He had mentioned to his brother, Ike, and Ike's wife, Winnie, that I needed a doctor. He told them what he had found on the Internet regarding my medicines, so I needed a new doctor soon. The doctors who had been treating me in Houston stopped seeing me because I had moved to a different state, and they no longer could accept my insurance. Ike and Winnie gave Will the name and phone number of their family physician and told Will to give him a call. They said what a wonderful doctor he was and that they were very pleased with him.

The next morning Will called their doctor, and the nurse informed us that he would see me as a new patient. Finally we were getting somewhere. We were so grateful. Finding a doctor was difficult, and it took a long time to find the right one. I guess with all my existing problems as a result of the brain surgery, most doctors didn't want to take on the liability. I understood completely.

Meeting a new doctor wasn't anything out of the ordinary for me. Since the brain surgery, I had seen hundreds of physicians. Seeing a new doctor just meant that I was going to be busy filling out a lot of paperwork, answering a million and one questions, and most likely having more tests. The doctor probably would want me to get another MRI and, of course, more blood work. My arms had a lot of scarring from all the blood tests and IVs so it was hard for them to draw blood at times. I prayed that this doctor would help me get off some of the medications, at least half of them. I never imagined what was about to happen.

When Dr. Sonier came in, I knew he was different. He didn't look or even act like the other doctors I had seen. He was young and tall, and his hair was long and curly. As he walked in the doorway, he smiled and stuck his hand out to shake ours. He had such a pleasant disposition. As he sat down, he began to ask me questions, and as I talked, he listened to me. It seemed like he was really interested in what I had to say, and he never rushed us when we spoke. He made me feel important. I knew he was going to be my doctor and that I could trust him.

Will told him, "Dr. Sonier, the reason we came in to see you today is for Casey. She had a tumor removed from her brain about fourteen years ago. It was on the left side of her cerebellum. She has been seeing several doctors in Houston, Texas, for the past few years, but now that she has moved back to Louisiana, she needs a doctor in this state."

"I understand," said Dr. Sonier.

In my Father's Land

"And Doctor," Will continued as he began digging into the bag of medications he had brought, "she suffers from grand mal seizures."

"How often do the seizures occur?" the doctor asked.

"She is having at least one or two a day. They don't last long, but it's every day," Will told him.

Dr. Sonier looked at me and asked, "Casey, do your hands and head tremble like this all the time?"

"Yes sir, most of the time," I replied. "And I get horrible headaches."

As Will was handing him the twenty-eight bottles of pills, he began to tell the doctor about my recent stay in the hospital with pneumonia.

"Casey, do you smoke?" asked the doctor.

"No sir, not anymore," I said.

"Good deal! I would like to get an X-ray of your lungs and also a new MRI of your brain."

Will had given Dr. Sonier all the bottles of medication I was taking, and he told the doctor what he had found out about the medications on the Internet. The doctor took out his Blackberry phone and started looking up each one. He was impressed with Will and all of the research he had done. To tell you the truth, I was quite impressed with Will too. I hadn't realized how much research he had actually done.

"Casey," Dr. Sonier said, "I want to take you off a few of these medications starting today. We are going to gradually stop them until you are completely off of them."

"Are you going to take me off all of the pills?" I asked.

"No," he said, "just a few to see how you react. Casey, you have been on these medications for a long time so it's going to take a while to get you off. There are some that you might never get off like the seizure and depression medications."

I remember leaving there with a whole new outlook on life, as if I might have some sort of a normal life that didn't revolve around doctors, hospitals, and medication. I went from taking twenty-eight pills a day to fourteen a day in a matter of a few months. I was feeling a lot better; the seizures were almost gone, and the headaches were few and far between. After three years I was down to ten pills a day, and three of those were nonprescription!

I told Will that I thought the medications I was taking were making me sick again. I didn't want to take them anymore.

"Will?" I said.

"Yes, Casey? What is it?"

"I think my medicine is making me sick. Every morning after I take it, I get sick to my stomach and can't get out of bed."

"Are you eating before you take your pills?" Will asked.

"Yes, I eat something, but that isn't it. It feels like I'm taking poison. I think I'm going to stop taking them."

"Casey, you can't just stop taking your medicines. You have to talk to the doctor. What if we try taking one pill out at a time until we find out which one is causing the problems?"

"Well, it's not like I can go see Dr. Sonier right now, so maybe you're right. I'll try leaving one pill out at a time and see what happens."

At the time Will had taken a job, working with his brother, Ike, in Iowa. I had followed him up there. Of course Dr. Sonier was back in Louisiana. So we decided to leave one pill out at a time for a couple of days to see how it would affect me, but nothing seemed to work. I was still sick. I couldn't lift my head up without puking. My stomach cramped badly as if I had food poisoning.

After a while, when nothing helped, I told Will no more medication.

"That's it," I said. I decided not to take them anymore. I knew Will was worried about what might happen if I suddenly stopped taking my medications. Dr. Sonier had warned me not to just stop taking any of them. So I prayed and ask God to help me, I was determined to stop. I wasn't going to lie in bed sick for another day. Will started helping me slowly get off one pill at a time. He watched me to see if I had any bad reaction. But my health began to improve, and within a couple of days, I was up and doing my everyday chores.

When we got back home, I went to see Dr. Sonier and told him what I had done. I have to tell you, he wasn't too happy that I had stopped taking my medication without consulting him. But since I had already done it, he wanted me to let him know if I started feeling bad or if I had a seizure. If that happened, Dr. Sonier wanted me to go to the nearest hospital and call him immediately! But, praise God, to this day I'm happy to say I don't take any medication. I'm very thankful to God for hearing and answering all of my prayers, for not only healing my body but also for healing my mind and my spirit. I thank God for the amazing people he put into my life who have stood by me through some really tough times, for the people who never gave up on me, and for the prayer warriors who stood in the gap; they never ceased in prayer.

Chapter 16

Because of God's healing, my memory is much better now and it's getting better with every passing day. It's incredible how clear my thoughts are. When I look back at all the things I have gone through, I'm truly amazed. There have been so many challenges and obstacles since the brain surgery, but with God's grace and mercy, I have made it through each and every one of them. I believe that because of the things I saw in heaven when I died, my life changed for the better. Somehow it made me a stronger and more loving person. I now look at situations in a different light. Some of the things that used to make me upset or feel down in the dumps don't anymore. It's just not that big of a deal. There are more important things in life to think about.

I know I have God to turn to when there is something bothering me. I don't seem to be so quick to judge people. I realize that is God's job to do, not mine. Now I'm not saying by any means that I'm perfect. I'm not, but God's not through with me yet. Let's just say I'm a work in progress! I find pleasure in the little things that this world has to offer. I take more time to listen to people, really listen to them. I enjoy the time I have with my family and friends more. We aren't on this earth forever, so I'm going to enjoy my family and friends for as long as God lets me.

I believe going to heaven and being in the presence of God changed my life for the better and forever. My attitude has changed toward everything and everyone, I have found forgiveness, and I'm more willing to walk away from strife when in the past I would stand and fight. Even though I couldn't stay in heaven, I brought a piece of heaven back with me. It's inside me; it's in my heart and in my soul. I think that's because I know one day I'll get back to heaven, and next time maybe I'll get to stay.

I have written down some of the Bible verses that my aunt Honey showed me when I came home from the hospital. I hope these verses help with any questions you might have. I truly hope this book is a blessing to you, and I pray that when you finish it, you will gain a peace and the understanding that God is waiting for you in heaven. There is nothing to be afraid of. Remember, God is love! So until we meet in heaven, God bless.

***

These scriptures come from the New King James Version of the Holy Bible:

Genesis 28:15 "Behold, I am with you and will keep you wherever you go, and will bring you back to this land; for I will not leave you until I have done what I have spoken to you."

This scripture helped me to know that God would make sure I was going to be okay, and he gave me a promise that he would never leave me.

Psalm 23: A Psalm of David "The Lord is my shepherd: I shall not want."

My auntie would recite this psalm. It gave me comfort, knowing that even though things didn't look good for me at the time, I didn't have to fear.

Psalm 46 "God is our refuge and strength."

Sometimes I felt as if the pain was never going to end. God told me in Psalm 46 that he was my refuge and my strength; all I had to do was lean on him.

Psalm 56:3 "Whenever I am afraid, I will trust in You."

This psalm has carried me through life in general. I have quoted Psalm 56 many times. It reminds me to put my faith in God and not in the situation at hand.

Psalm 56:8 "You number my wanderings; Put my tears into your bottle; Are they not in Your book?"

He knows where we are, and he knows every tear that we cry. He bottles our tears. He knows all about our lives!

Psalm 73:28 "But it is good for me to draw near to God; I have put my trust in the Lord God, That I may declare all Your works."

No matter where you are, remember to draw near to God for he loves you and will always be there for you. Always!

Psalm 126:5 "Those who sow in tears, Shall reap in joy."

This is so awesome! God lets us know that our sorrow won't last forever.

Psalm 130 "Lord, hear my voice!"

Reading this verse let me know that I wasn't the only one that cried out to the Lord. It was reassurance that God hears our prayers.

Psalm 143:7–8 Depression

Because I fought such bad depression, I was glad that the illness is talked about in the Bible.

Proverbs 14:27 "The fear of the Lord is a fountain of life, To turn one away from the snares of death."

I never wanted God to be upset with me. The Bible talks about God's wrath, and I promised him I would write this book while I was in the hospital, so I was going to keep that promise.

Isaiah 25:8 "He will swallow up death forever, And the Lord God will wipe away tears from all faces; the rebuke of His people He will take away from all the earth; For the Lord has spoken."

I took comfort in knowing that God was going to wipe away my tears, every single one of them.

Isaiah 41:10 "Fear not, for I am with you; Be not dismayed, for I am your God. I will strengthen you, yes I will help you. I will uphold you with my righteous right hand."

As I have said before, there were times in my life when I was fearful, but as you see in this verse, God tells us that he will strengthen us and that he will uphold us.

Daniel 9:8–10 O Lord, to us belongs shame of face, to our kings, our princes, and our father, because we have sinned against You. 9 To the Lord our God belong mercy and forgiveness, though we have rebelled against Him. 10 We have not obeyed the voice of the Lord our God, to walk in His laws, which He set before us by His servants the prophets.

I love Daniel. God has mercy even for the ones who are rebellious.

Malachi 4:2 "But to you who fear My name The Sun of Righteousness shall arise with healing in His wings; And you shall go out And grow fat like stall-fed calves."

I believed that God was going to heal me; he said he would.

Matthew 4:23 Healing

I loved to read about how Jesus healed all kinds of sicknesses and all kinds of diseases. So I knew he could heal me.

Matthew 6:7–13 The Lord tells us how to pray.

Like many people I always wanted to know if I was praying correctly. In this verse the Lord tells us how to pray. I know the Lord's Prayer by heart. It means so much to me. It gives me comfort. I pray that everyone will learn it and take comfort in it too.

Mark 3:28–29 "All sins will be forgiven" except for "he who blasphemes against the Holy Spirit."

God promises to forgive us of all of our sins.

John 3:16 "For God so loved the world that He gave His only begotten Son, that whoever believes in Him should not perish but have everlasting life."

That is God's promise to all of us who believe in him.

Colossians 1:14 Forgiveness of sins through his blood

Only through Jesus's death and the shedding of his blood were we redeemed.

1 Corinthians 15:55–58 Death

In Corinthians it says that Jesus took the sting out of death. It says that death is swallowed up in victory. The Bible says the sting of death is sin and that strength of sin is the law. But thanks be to God, who gives us the victory through our Lord Jesus Christ.

2 Corinthians 2:14 Aroma

The Bible talks about the "fragrance of His knowledge" being in every place.

2 Corinthians 2:15 "For we are to God the fragrance of Christ among those who are being saved and among those who are perishing."

I smelled a wonderful scent when I was on the staircase to heaven, and this verse talks about that sweet savor.

Ephesians 1:2-14 Our inheritance as believers in Christ

This scripture talks about the many spiritual blessings that God has given us "through His blood, the forgiveness of sins, according to the riches of His grace."

Ephesians 6:8 "Knowing that whatever good anyone does, he will receive that same from the Lord, whether he is a slave or free."

If we follow the word of God. Then we know to do all things with Love. I want love to come back to me, therefore I try and show love.

Ephesians 6:10–20 The whole armor of God

This is truly one of my favorite scriptures. God gives us his armor to protect ourselves. I think we should do this every day.

Hebrews 5:7 "Who, in the days of His flesh, when He had offered up prayers and supplications, with vehement cries and tears to Him who was able to save Him from death, and was heard because of His godly fear."

I knew God heard my cries and I knew that he heard me and would not forsake me.

Revelation 5:8 "Now when He had taken the scroll, the four living creatures and the twenty-four elders fell down before the Lamb, each having a harp, and golden bowls full of incense, which are the prayers of the saints."

I smelled a wonderful aroma when I was on the staircase. It says here that the prayers of the saints are of incense.

Revelation 21 "Now I saw a new heaven and a new earth, for the first heaven and the first earth had passed away."

When I asked my dad why he was dressed for work, he told me he was working on the new world that God was making. This confirmed what my dad said to me.

About the Author

My name is Rhonda Powell After dying during brain surgery, I made God a promise, that I would let everyone know that there is life after death. That God is waiting for us up in Heaven. I'm a Christian. And a mother to 3 children. They have seen me struggle through many obstacle's in my life, But they have also seen God deliver me from every one of them. I was born in a small Town in Southern Texas. Where our belief in God came before any and everything. I want everyone to know that they don't have to fear death. God is there. He is waiting.

Made in United States
Orlando, FL
04 January 2022